PESACH

פֶּסַח

A Holiday Funtext

by Judy Bin-Nun

with Nancy Cooper

and

Ruth Sternfeld

illustrated by Heidi Steinberger

Union of American Hebrew Congregations

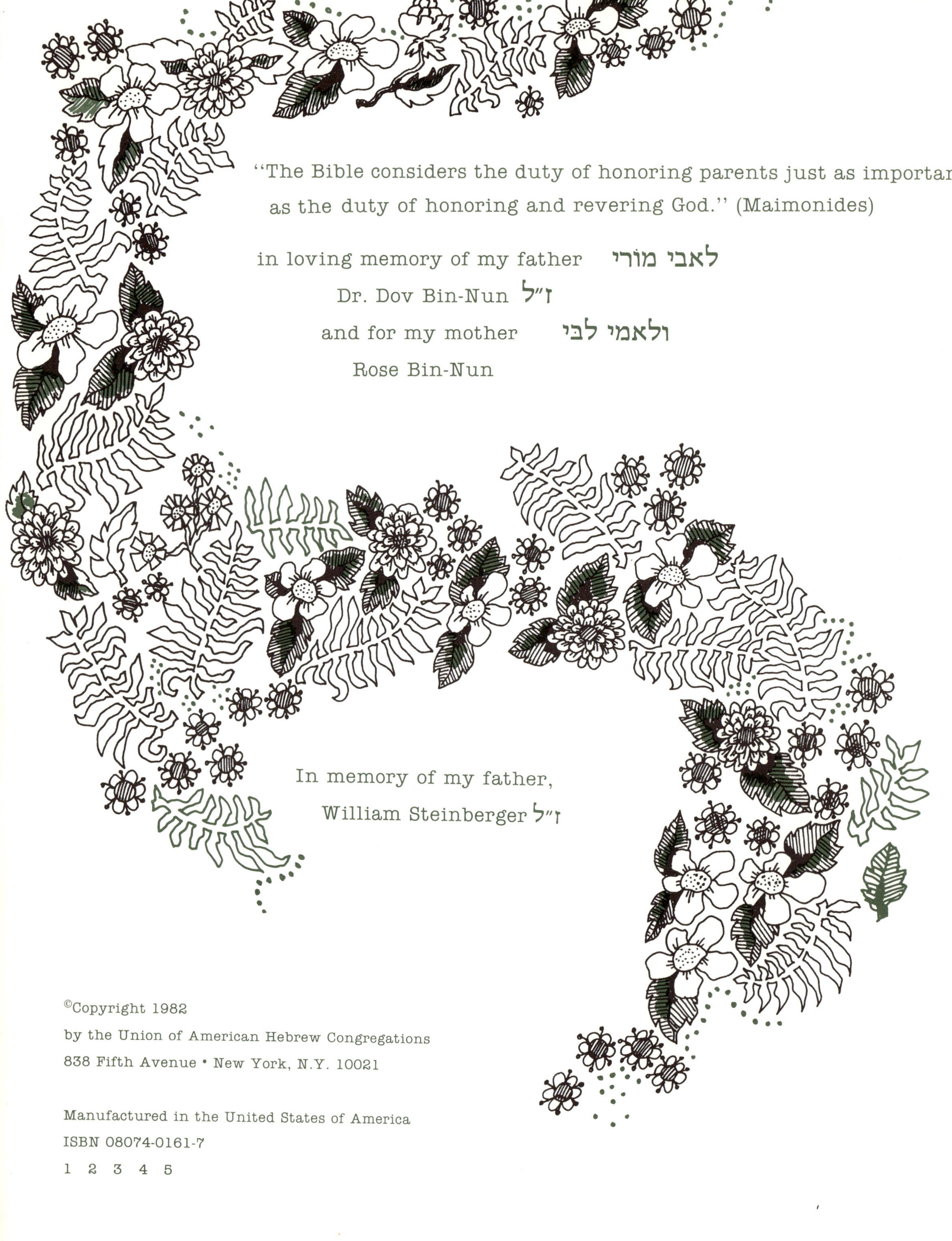

"The Bible considers the duty of honoring parents just as important as the duty of honoring and revering God." (Maimonides)

in loving memory of my father לאבי מורי
Dr. Dov Bin-Nun ז"ל
and for my mother ולאמי לבי
Rose Bin-Nun

In memory of my father,
William Steinberger ז"ל

838 Fifth Avenue • New York, N.Y. 10021

Manufactured in the United States of America
ISBN 08074-0161-7
1 2 3 4 5

SHALOM! שָׁלוֹם

This is a book about *Pesach* (פֶּסַח), Passover, the Jewish spring festival of freedom. *Pesach* is also called *Zeman Cherutenu* (זְמַן חֵרוּתֵנוּ), the Season of Our Freedom.

We're going to learn how and why Jewish people, just like you, celebrate *Pesach* and enjoy its special customs.

ACTIVITY CODE

Look at the code and follow the directions on every page.

Look — Draw

Read — Imagine, think

Circle — Match

Color — Follow the dots

Cut — Write

PASTE

Paste

HAVE FUN!

BEING FREE

Being free means different things to different people. Freedom means you have a choice. Freedom means you must know what is right and what is wrong. And, when you make a choice, you can't think just about yourself; you also have to think about the feelings of other people.

Circle the pictures that mean being free to you.

My favorite free time activity

Being me is like being free!

A long time ago in a country named Egypt, the Jewish people were not free. They could not choose how they wanted to live or work. The king of Egypt (called Pharaoh) made the Jewish people his slaves. The slaves worked very hard for a very long time and did not have time to rest.

The Jewish people hated being slaves. They prayed to God to free them from slavery in Egypt. So, the Torah says, Moses came to Egypt to help save the Jewish people from their sad life.

The Jewish people were slaves to Pharaoh in Egypt.

THE TEN PLAGUES

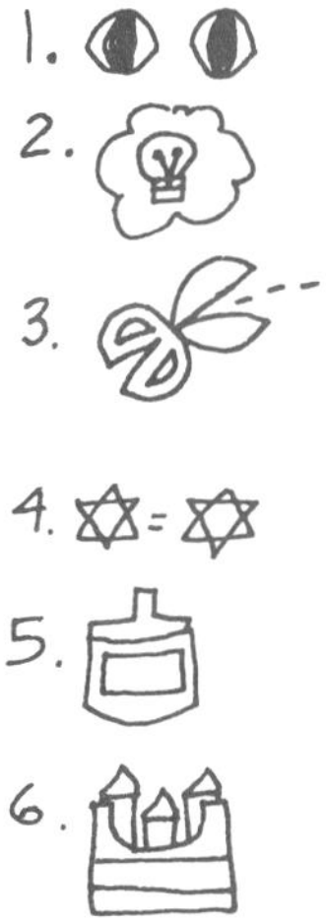

Ten plagues were brought upon Pharaoh and all Egypt. The plagues were strange and scary. The Egyptians became so angry and unhappy that they told Pharaoh to stop the plagues and set the Jewish people free.

Below are the ten plagues. Each plague has a different shape. Cut out the plague shapes and match them with the same shapes on page 9.

2.

3.

MATCHING THE PLAGUES

Here are the ten shapes to help you remember the ten plagues.
Paste the plague shapes from page 7 on the shapes below.

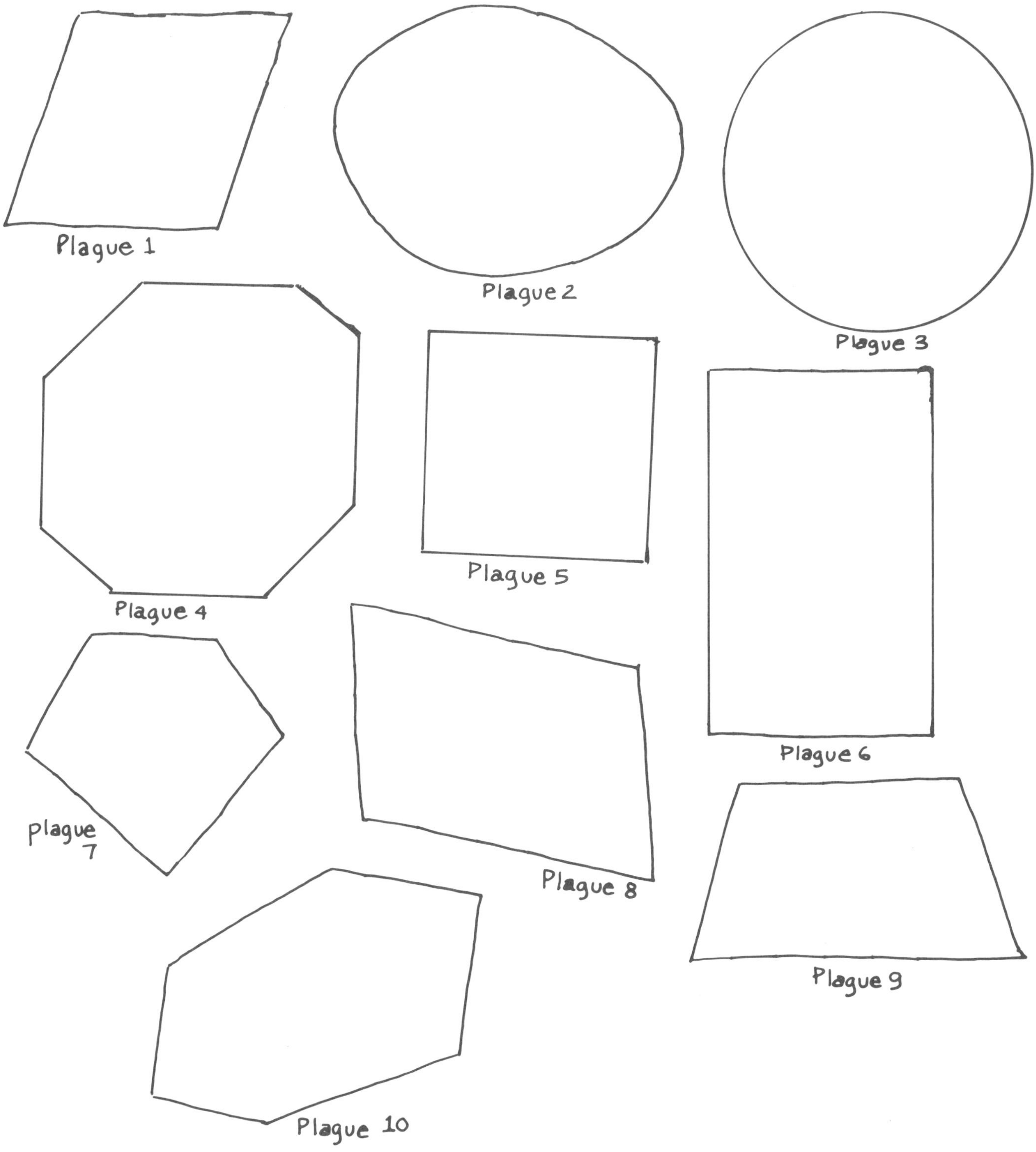

Plague 1

Plague 2

Plague 3

Plague 4

Plague 5

Plague 6

Plague 7

Plague 8

Plague 9

Plague 10

1. 

2. 

3.

4. 

MAKING OUR HOMES SPECIAL FOR PESACH

To make the home special for *Pesach*, Jewish families clean their homes and get rid of all foods called "*chametz*" (חָמֵץ).

Chametz is food made with flours that rise. We do not eat *chametz* for the whole week of *Pesach*. We eat *matzah* and special *Pesach* foods instead. Each time we eat *matzah* and other *Pesach* foods, it is good to remember that long ago we were slaves in Egypt and today we are free.

On the night before *Pesach*, you can look for *chametz* in your home. Some Jewish people search for *chametz* using a candle, a feather, and a wooden spoon. The candle lights the way and the feather sweeps the *chametz* into the wooden spoon.

You can use your pencil to circle the *chametz* hidden in the house below.

MEALTIME AT YOUR HOME

What do you think makes a meal special?
Is it the food ?
Is it how the table is set ?
Could it be the clothes you wear ?
Or the way your family gets together and talks ?
Maybe you even sing or play games at your mealtime.

On the empty table below, draw a picture of *your* most special meal. Don't forget to put your family into your picture.

At *Pesach*, we have two special dinner meals. We call the special *Pesach* meal a *seder* (סֵדֶר). The word *seder* means "order" in Hebrew.

You have an order of things to do during and after the *seder* meal. On page 13 you learn about the 14 parts of a *Pesach seder*.

*   *   *   *   *   *   *

Before the order of the *seder* starts,
We remember a symbol that gladdens our hearts.
What is blessed first in your holiday home?

The symbol you will come to know,
By following the dots you see below.*

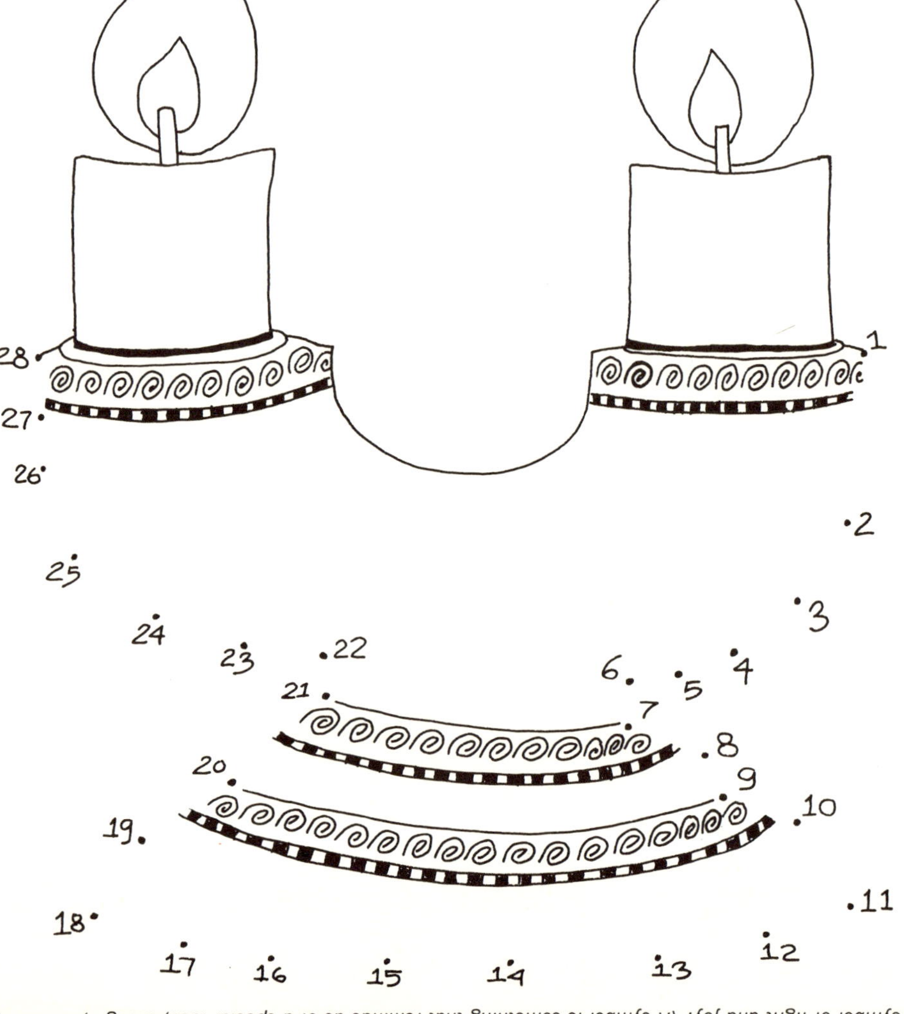

*Did you find candles, the symbol of light and joy? (A symbol is something that reminds us of a special idea, thought, or feeling.)

Let all who are hungry come and eat.

At the *seder* meal, we read from a book  called a *Haggadah* (הַגָּדָה). The *Haggadah* helps us follow the right order for our *Pesach* celebration. The *Haggadah* also tells the *Pesach* story and has special songs, readings, and *berachot* for the holiday.

Following is a cover you can use to decorate your *Haggadah.* We have written in Hebrew *Haggadah shel Pesach* (Passover *Haggadah*); now you decorate the rest.

Cut out this *Haggadah* cover and attach it with paper clips  or tape  to your own *Haggadah.* Use your *Haggadah* at your family *seder.*

MY OWN HAGGADAH COVER

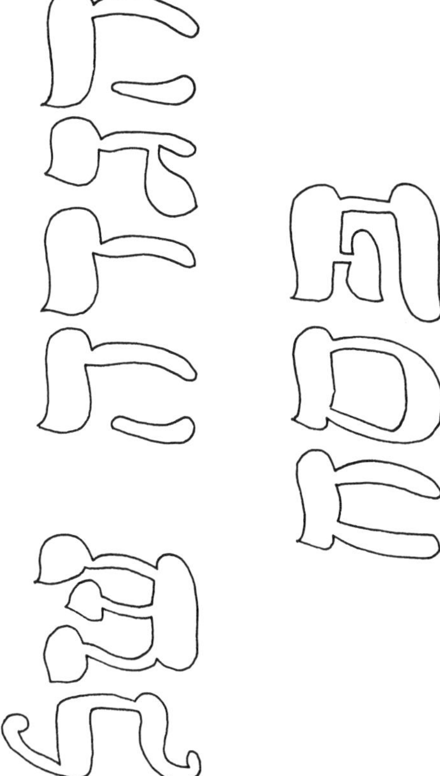

1. 2. 3.

WHY IS THIS NIGHT DIFFERENT?
THE FOUR QUESTIONS

There is a part of the *seder* which is special for children. You get to ask the people at your *seder* the Four *Pesach* Questions.

Here are the Four Questions. Circle the picture that matches the question.

1. Why is this night different from all other nights? On this night we eat *matzah* and not other kinds of bread. Why?

2. On this night we must eat a bitter vegetable. Why?

3. On this night we must dip our food in two things. On other nights we don't need to dip our food at all. Why?

4. On this night we lean on pillows instead of sitting up straight in our chairs.

On other nights we don't sit like this.

Why?

In every age, Jewish people must think of themselves as having come out of ancient Egypt. Here are the answers to the Four *Pesach* Questions. Match the answers with the number of the right question on page 17.

This answer goes with question number_____

We lean on pillows at our *seder* to show how we are free and not slaves. We can relax and celebrate *Pesach*.

This answer goes with question number_____

We eat *matzah* to remember that once we were slaves in Egypt. The slaves did not have time to bake real bread.

This answer goes with question number_____

We dip our vegetable once in salt water to taste the tears of the Jewish slaves. Later, we dip our bitter vegetable in *charoset* to remind us of the sadness of slavery and the sweetness of freedom.

This answer goes with question number_____

We eat bitter vegetables to help us understand the sad and bitter feelings of the Jewish people when they were slaves in Egypt.

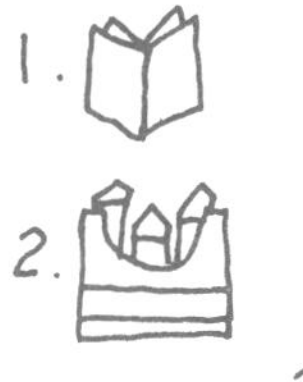

An important part of the *Pesach seder* is the *seder* plate, *ke'arat Pesach* (קְעָרַת פֶּסַח).

On this plate are six different foods. They are symbols of the holiday. You will remember that a symbol is something that reminds us of a special idea, thought, or feeling.

Each of the foods on the *seder* plate is a symbol and has its own *Pesach* meaning. Come and meet each *Pesach* symbol and find out why it is special for your holiday celebration.

KARPAS— כַּרְפַּס

This is *karpas*—parsley or greens. *Karpas* is the symbol of spring when everything starts to grow again.

ZEROA— זְרוֹעַ

This is *zeroa*—a roasted shankbone. *Zeroa* is the symbol of the lamb sacrifice made during *Pesach* long ago.

CHAROSET— חֲרוֹסֶת

This is *charoset*—a mixture of chopped apples, nuts, and wine. *Charoset* is the symbol of the bricks made by the Jewish slaves for Pharaoh's buildings.

MAROR— מָרוֹר

This is *maror*—a bitter vegetable like horseradish. *Maror* tastes bitter. *Maror* is the symbol of the bitter and hard life of the Jewish slaves in Egypt.

BETZAH— בֵּיצָה

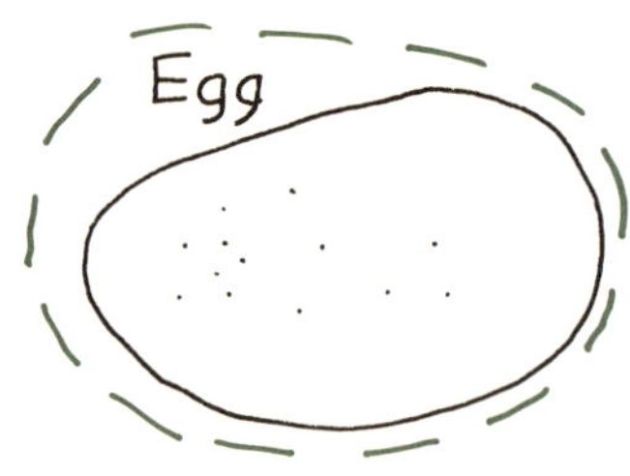

This is *betzah*—a roasted egg. *Betzah* is a symbol of life.

MEI MELACH— מֵי מֶלַח

This is *mei melach*—salt water. *Mei melach* is the symbol of all the tears cried by the Jewish slaves in Egypt.

Here are two more *Pesach* symbols on your *seder* table.

MATZAH— מַצָּה

This is *matzah.* The *matzah* reminds us that the Jews left Egypt in a hurry and did not have time to bake bread properly.

KOS ELIYAHU— כּוֹס אֵלִיָּהוּ

This is *Kos Eliyahu*—Elijah's Cup. Elijah was a famous Jewish prophet or wise man in biblical times. We remember Elijah at *Pesach* by a special wine cup put on the table in his honor.

1. 

2. 

3. 

4. 

MAKE YOUR OWN SEDER PLATE

Cut out the food symbols on pages 19 and 20 and paste them in the matching spaces to make a complete *seder* plate.

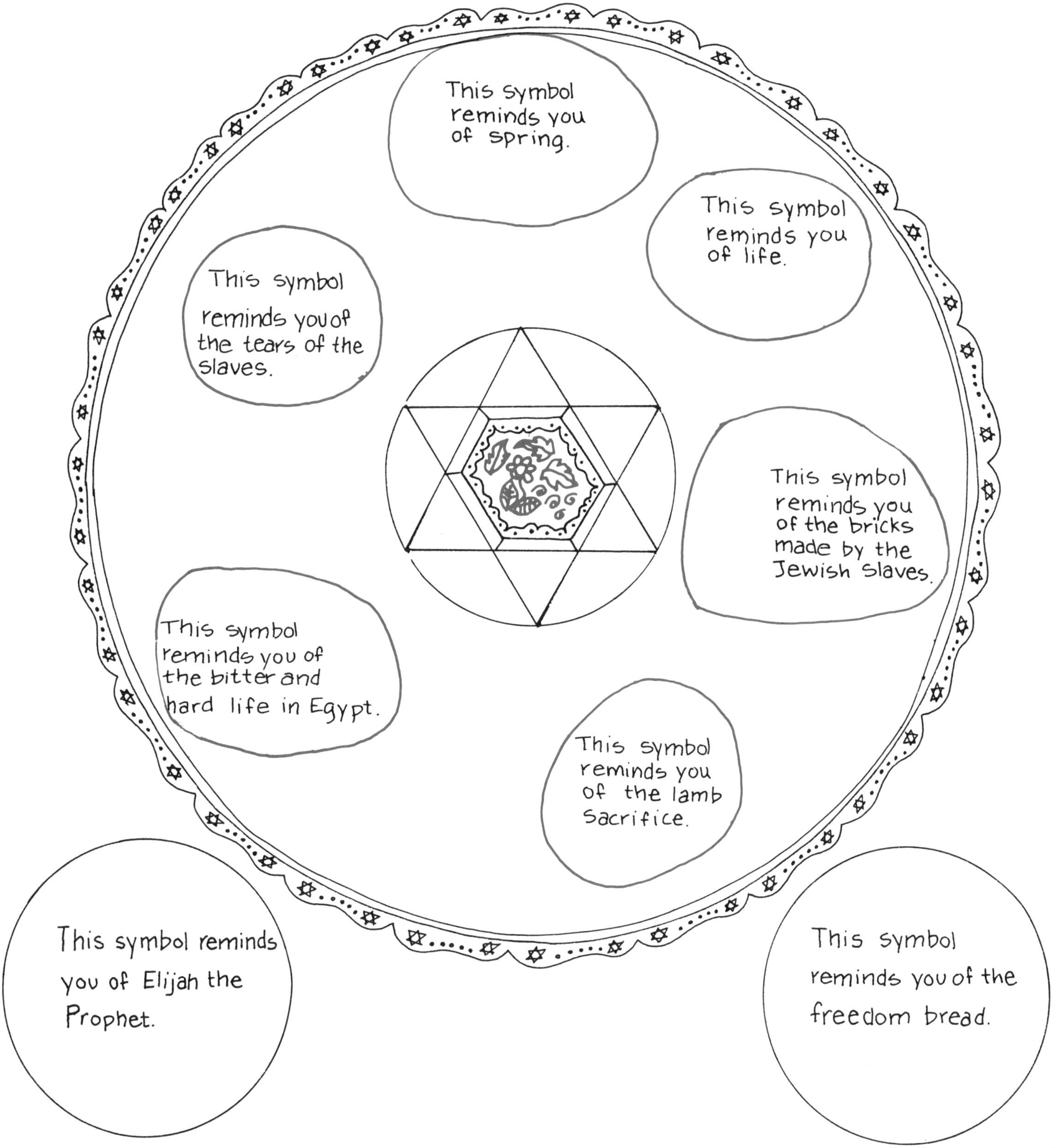

This symbol reminds you of spring.

This symbol reminds you of life.

This symbol reminds you of the tears of the slaves.

This symbol reminds you of the bricks made by the Jewish slaves.

This symbol reminds you of the bitter and hard life in Egypt.

This symbol reminds you of the lamb sacrifice.

This symbol reminds you of Elijah the Prophet.

This symbol reminds you of the freedom bread.

Blessings, *berachot* (בְּרָכוֹת) in Hebrew, help us to thank God for many good things. Here are the *berachot* just for *Pesach*.

After reading the *Pesach berachot*, by drawing a line, match each *berachah* with the picture it tells about.

Blessed are You, our God, Ruler of the universe, Creator of the fruit that grows on the vine (the grapes that are made into *wine*).
Baruch Atah Adonai, Elohenu Melech haolam, Boray peri hagafen.

Blessed are You, our God, Ruler of the universe, who has made us special through commandments, especially the commandment of eating the freedom cakes called *matzah.*
Baruch Atah Adonai, Elohenu Melech haolam, asher kideshanu bemitzvotov vetzivanu al achilat matzah.

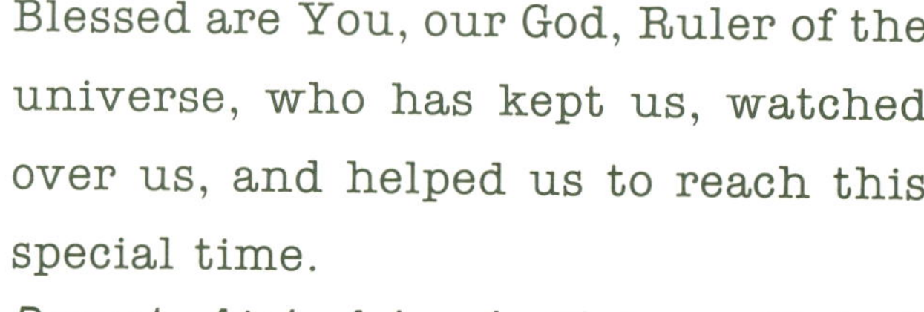

Blessed are You, our God, Ruler of the universe, who has kept us, watched over us, and helped us to reach this special time.
Baruch Atah Adonai, Elohenu Melech haolam, shehecheyanu, vekiyemanu, vehigiyanu lazeman hazeh.

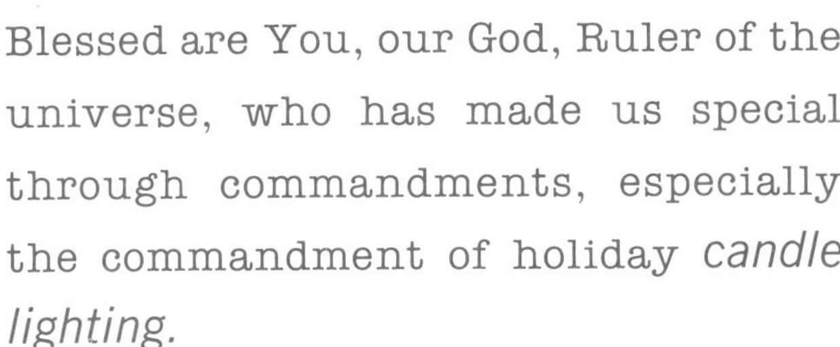

Blessed are You, our God, Ruler of the universe, who has made us special through commandments, especially the commandment of holiday *candle lighting.*

Baruch Atah Adonai, Elohenu Melech haolam, asher kideshanu bemitzvotav vetzivanu lehadlik ner shel yom tov.

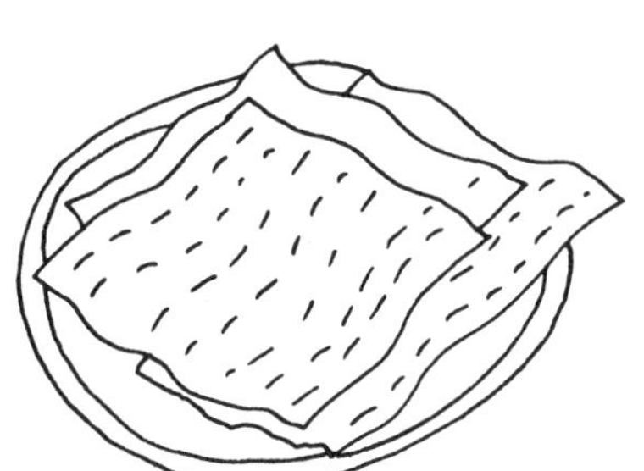

Blessed are You, our God, Ruler of the universe, who has made us special through commandments, especially the commandment of eating a *bitter vegetable.*

Baruch Atah Adonai, Elohenu Melech haolam, asher kideshanu bemitzvotav vetzivanu al achilat maror.

Blessed are You, our God, Ruler of the universe, who gave us the *bread* we eat.

Baruch Atah Adonai, Elohenu Melech haolam, hamotzi lechem min ha'aretz.

Blessed are You, our God, Ruler of the universe, Creator of the *green vegetables* which are grown in the earth.

Baruch Atah Adonai, Elohenu Melech haolam, Boray peri ha'adamah.

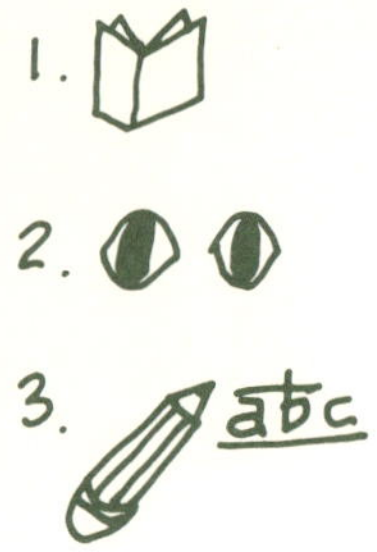

FIND THE AFIKOMAN

During our *Pesach seder,* we play a special game with the second *matzah* on our *matzah* plate. The leader of the *seder* breaks the second *matzah* in half and then hides it somewhere in the home. This *matzah* is called the *afikoman*(אֲפִיקוֹמָן). After dinner everyone tries to find the *afikoman* because it is needed to finish the *seder* meal. The *afikoman* is our official dessert. The person who finds the *afikoman* gets a prize.

Help find the *afikoman* in time for dessert without crossing any lines.

The *afikoman* treat
Makes your *seder* complete.

1. 

FOLLOW THE DOTS . . .

2. 

. . .to meet the star
Of a *Pesach* song called "*Chad Gadya.*"

3. 

4. 

At the *seder* there will be
This favorite song about *gedi.*

Connect the dots so you can see
What in Hebrew we call *gedi.**

An only kid, an only kid,
My father bought for 2 zuzim.
An only kid! An only kid!

Chad gadya, chad gadya,
Dezabin abba biteray zuzay.
Chad gadya! Chad gadya!

*Did you find a little kid (goat)?

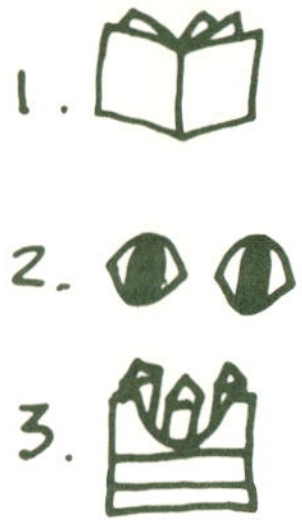

The Hebrew word, *dayenu* (דַּיֵּנוּ), means "It would have been enough for us." The song, *"Dayenu,"* tells about a lot of wonderful things that God did for the Jewish people.

Color *only* the spaces with dots to find three of the many special things* God gave to the Jewish people.

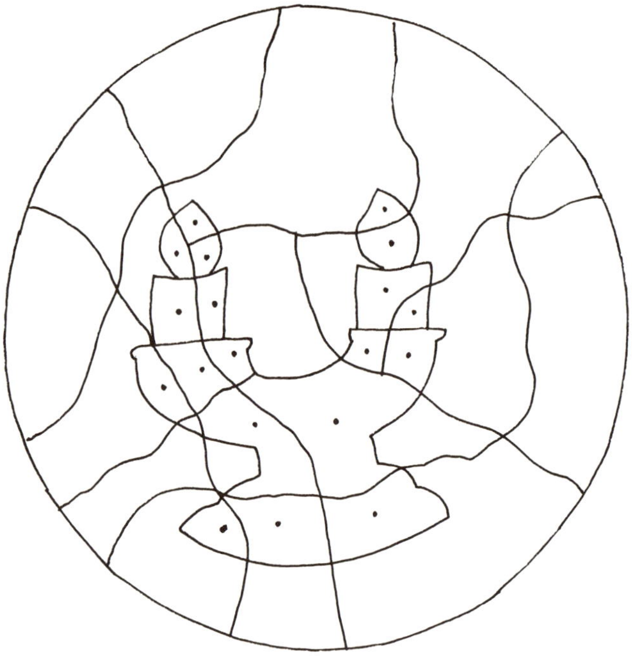

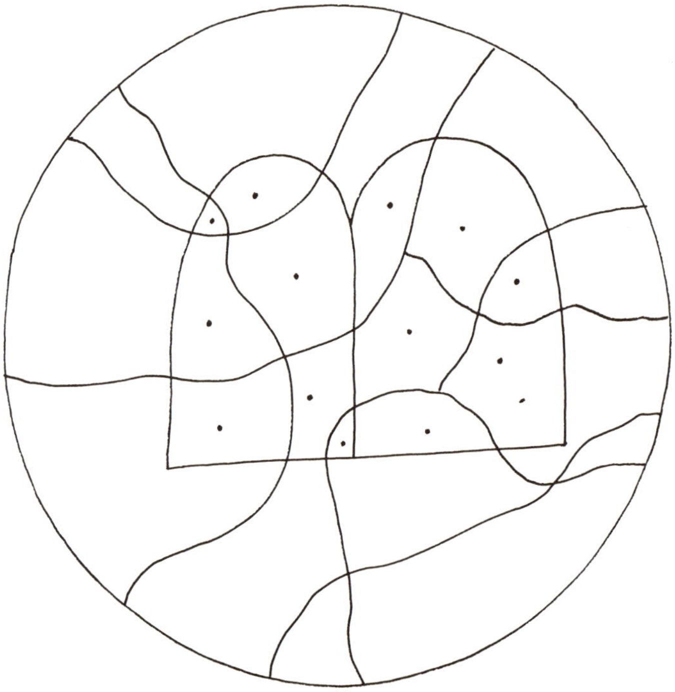

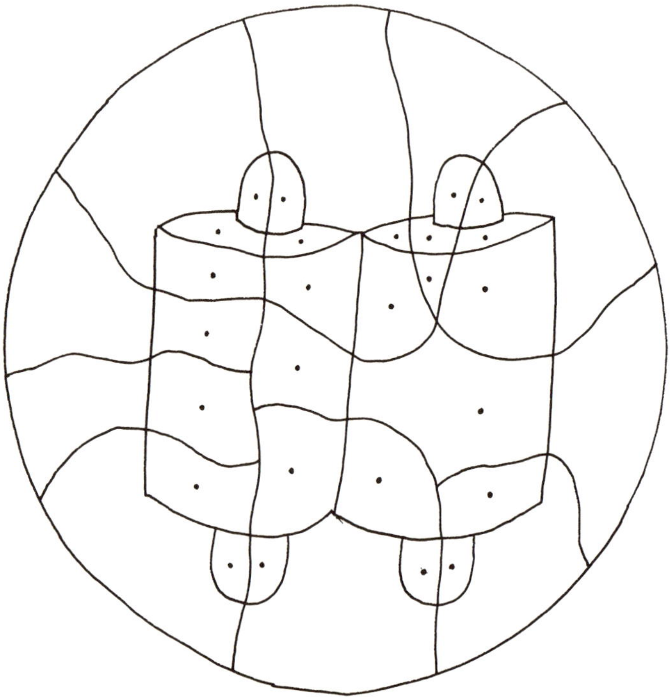

*Did you find a Torah, the Ten Commandments, and the Shabbat symbols?

WHO KNOWS ONE? "ECHAD MI YODEA?"—A PESACH NUMBERS SONG

We sing a counting song at our *Pesach seder* called "*Echad Mi Yodea*?"

Match the pictures with the verses below.

Who knows one? One is our God in heaven and on earth.

Who knows two? Two are the tables of the commandments.

Who knows three? Three is the number of the patriarchs.

Who knows four? Four is the number of the matriarchs.

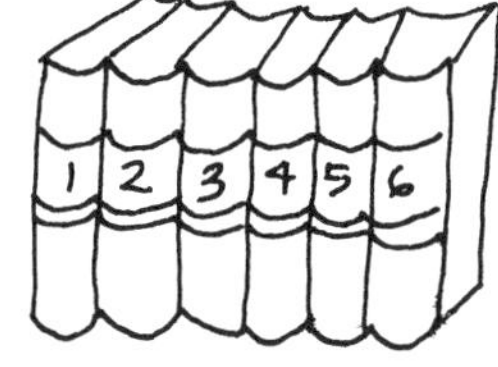

Who knows five? Five books there are in the Torah.

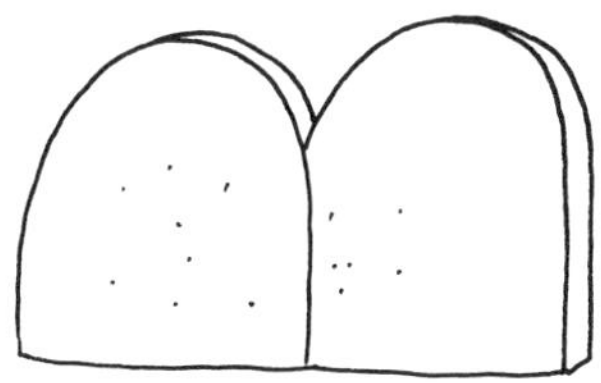

Who knows six? Six sections the Mishnah has.

Who knows seven? Seven days there are in a week.

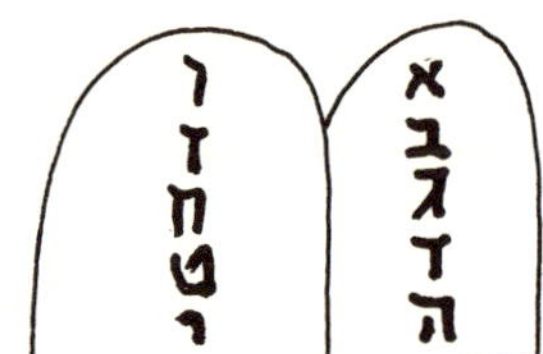

Who knows eight? Eight are the days to the service of the covenant.

Who knows nine? Nine is the number of the holidays.

Who knows ten? Ten commandments were given on Sinai.

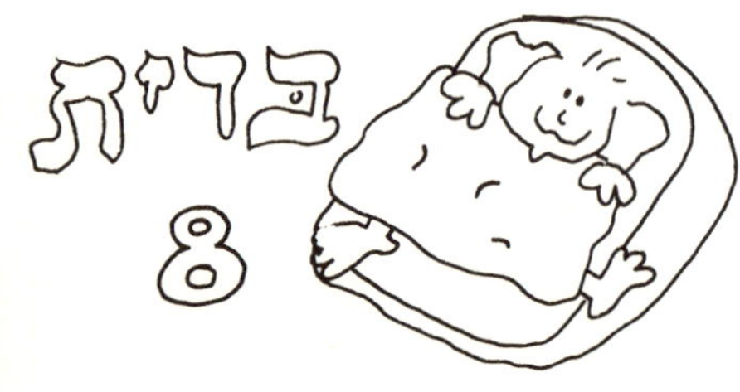

Who knows eleven? Eleven were the stars in Joseph's dream.

Who knows twelve? Twelve are the tribes of Israel.

SAT	SUN	MON	TUES	WED	THURS	FRI
1	2	3	4	5	6	7

Who knows thirteen? Thirteen are the attributes of God.

THE MAGICAL NUMBER 4

Look and see how the number 4 is used at the *Pesach seder.*

At the *seder,* we drink *4* cups of wine.

At the *seder,* we read the story of the *4* children.

At the *seder,* the youngest person asks the *4* Questions.

Why is this night different?

At the *seder,* we have *4 matzot* on a special plate.

The *matzot* are symbols.

1. the Kohen
2. the Levite
3. the Israelite

   and

4. the *matzah* of freedom

for all Jews who are still not free today.

DO NOT 4GET

THE MAGICAL NUMBER 4!

1. 

OUR SEDER IS OVER

2. 

Our *seder* helped to tell us the story of *Pesach*. At the *seder* we thought about Jewish life long ago.

At the end of our *seder* we say: "Next year in Jerusalem." We remember our love for the State of Israel—the land that the tired slaves dreamed of after they left Egypt.

לשנה הבאה
בירשלים

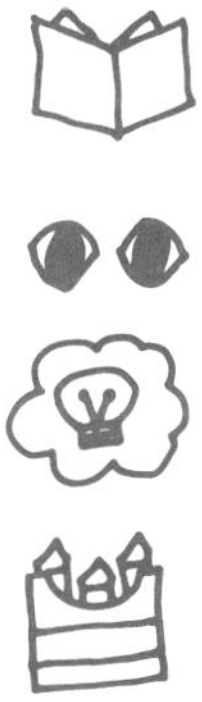

FIND THE HIDDEN PESACH SYMBOLS

matzah, Elijah's Cup, parsley (*karpas*), shankbone (*zeroa*), an only kid (*gedi*), roasted egg (*betzah*), bitter vegetable (*maror*), *Haggadah,* and holiday candlesticks.

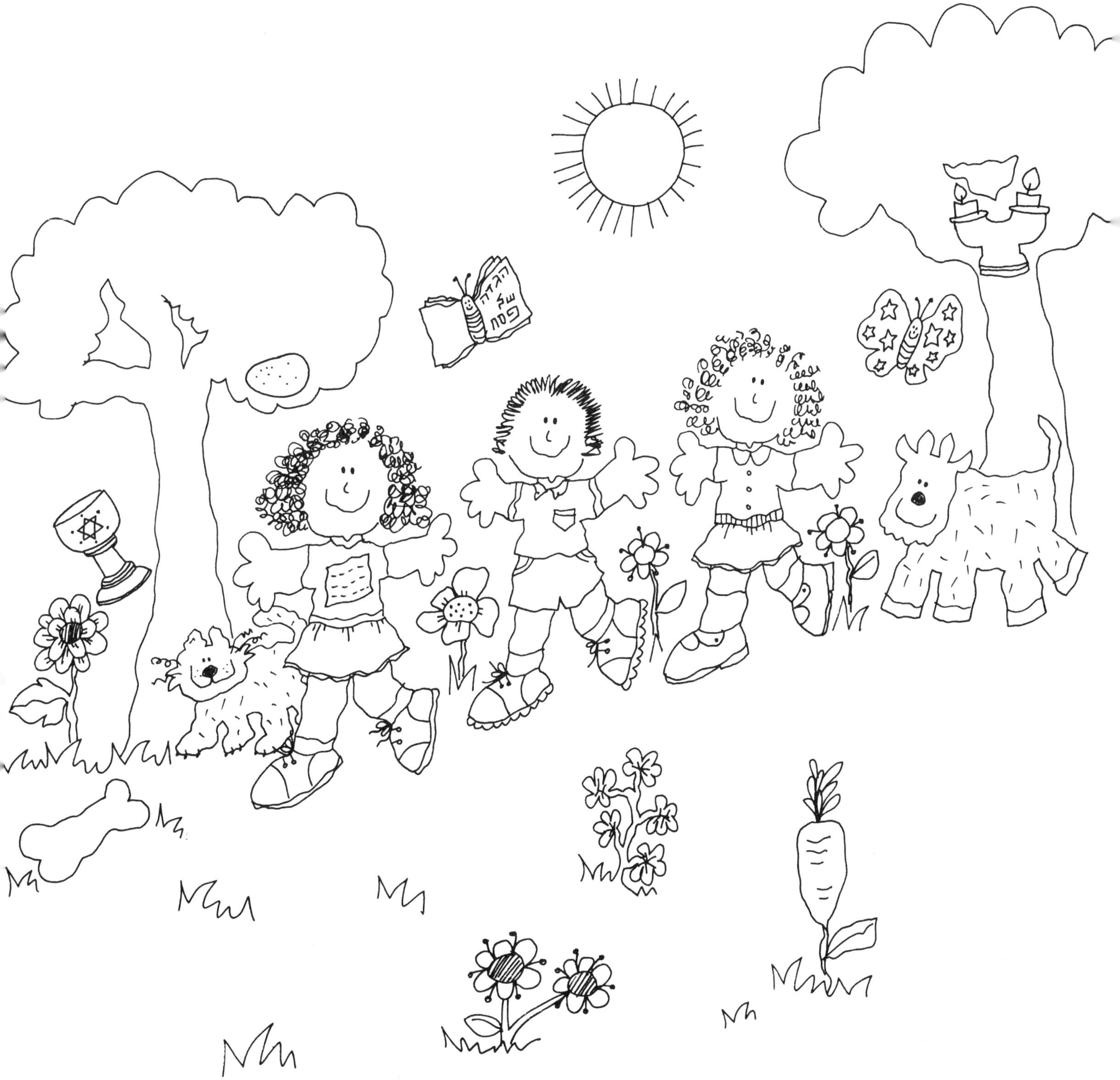

THANKS TO

SOME SPECIAL PEOPLE

Rabbi Daniel Syme, Rabbi Steven Reuben, Rabbi Howard Laibson, Rabbi David Katz, Rabbi Patrice Heller, Gerry Gould, Sandra Bernstein, Miriam Hurewitz, Kenneth Midlo